by

Theresa Rebeck

FOUNDED 1830

New York   Hollywood   London   Toronto

SAMUELFRENCH.COM

IMPORTANT BILLING AND CREDIT REQUIREMENTS

All producers of THE SCENE *must* give credit to the Author of the Play in all programs distributed in connection with performances of the Play, and in all instances in which the title of the Play appears for the purposes of advertising, publicizing or otherwise exploiting the Play and /or a production. The name of the Author *must* appear on a separate line on which no other name appears, immediately following the title and *must* appear in size of type not less than fifty percent of the size of the title type.

All licensees shall be required to give the following acknowledgement on the title page of all programs distributed in connection with the performance of the play:

Premiered in the 2006 Humana Festival of New American Plays at Actors Theatre of Louisville

Produced be Second Stage Theatre, New York, January 11, 2007 Carole Rothman, Artistic Director

2econd Stage Theatre

Carole Rothman *Artistic Director* Ellen Richard *Executive Director*

presents

THE SCENE

BY THERESA REBECK

WITH Anna Camp, Patricia Heaton,
Tony Shalhoub, Christopher Evan Welch

SET DESIGN BY
Derek McLane

COSTUME DESIGN BY
Jeff Mahshie

LIGHTING DESIGN BY
Natasha Katz

SOUND DESIGN BY
Martin Desjardins

PRESS
Richard Kornberg & Associates

CASTING
Tara Rubin Casting

PRODUCTION STAGE MANAGER
Kelly Hance

STAGE MANAGER
Shanna Spinello

Christopher Burney
Associate Artistic Director

Jeff Wild
Production Manager

DIRECTED BY
REBECCA TAICHMAN

MEDIA SPONSOR
WNYC

Second Stage Theatre wishes to express its appreciation to
Theatre Development Fund for its support of this production.

Premiered in the 2006 Humana Festival of New Plays at the Actors Theatre of Louisville.

THE SCENE opened on January 11, 2007 in New York at Second Stage Theatre, with the following cast:

CLEA..Anna Camp
STELLA..Patricia Heaton
CHARLIE...Tony Shalhoub
LEWIS.................................Christopher Evan Welch

THE SCENE premiered on March 11, 2006 at the Actors Theatre of Louisville, with the following cast:

CLEA..Anna Camp
STELLA..Carla Harting
CHARLIE..............................Stephen Barker Turner
LEWIS...................................David Wilson Barnes

ACT I

Scene 1

(CHARLIE, LEWIS and CLEA. A corner of a party, loud music, talk, laughter. Charlie and Lewis hold drinks in their hands. Lewis is clearly interested in Clea; Charlie is not.)

CLEA. I love the view here.

LEWIS. *(Surreptitiously checking out her butt.)* Awesome.

CLEA. I mean, mind blowing, right, it's just so surreal, the lights and the water, it's like unbelievable. I love this loft! Do you know the guy who lives here? He must be incredible. Because I have just no idea, I came with a friend, who knows, like, everybody and I know she told me it was somebody in the fashion industry who I just so had never heard of, my bad. 'Cause he's like, what, like clearly so talented, this place is so beautiful. The water, the air. It's just so surreal.

CHARLIE. How is that surreal?

CLEA. What?

CHARLIE. The air and the water, you said that before, that you found it surreal. How is air and water surreal?

CLEA. Oh you know, it's — just — wow! You know.

CHARLIE. *(To LEWIS, annoyed now.)* You want a refill? What is that, a mojito?

LEWIS. Yeah, great.

CHARLIE. How about you, I'm sorry, what's your name again?

CLEA. Clea.

CHARLIE. Would you like a mojita, Clea?

CLEA. No no, I don't drink. My mother was an alcoholic. I mean, she was a wonderful woman and she really loved me but it's like alcohol is so deadly, I mean at these parties sometimes when I'm at a party like this? To stand around and watch everyone turn into zombies around me? It just really triggers me, you know? You go ahead. I mean, that's just for me, I don't impose that on people or anything.

LEWIS. I mean, it's not like, I'm not like a huge drinker, or —

CLEA. Oh good, because you know, I was at this party last week it was such a scene, there were so many people there. You know it was this young director, he's got like seven things going at once, off broadway. Can you imagine, the energy level of someone like that? Anyway, it was his birthday party, and they rented out the top two floors of this loft in Chelsea, it was this wild party, like surreal, and then at one point in the evening? I just realized, that everyone was just totally shitfaced. I mean I don't want to be reactive in situations like that, I don't like to judge people on a really superficial level or anything but it was kind of horrifying. I mean, not that I — you know, drink, you should drink! Enjoy yourselves!

(LEWIS and CHARLIE look at their drinks.)

CHARLIE. Yeah, well, I think I'm gonna head out. Nice to meet you. "Clea."

CLEA. Oh. Whoa. I mean — what does that mean?

CHARLIE. *(Annoyed now.)* What does what mean?

CLEA. "Clea." I mean, "Clea." I mean, whoa —

CHARLIE. Is there a problem?

CLEA. You tell me. You're the one who's all like, "Clea." "Nice to meet you."

CHARLIE. What are you even talking about?

CLEA. Nothing. It just struck me as a little edgy, that's all.

LEWIS. You want me to get those drinks? Why don't I do that? I mean you got to at least talk to Nick, he's gonna show up.

CHARLIE. I'm not talking to Nick. I'm leaving. *(To CLEA.)* "Nice to meet you —" is "edgy —"

CLEA. Well, you're totally giving off a vibe here, I'm not making that up. And that is so fine, I mean I do not judge.

LEWIS. Look, Nick's here. Hey Nick —

CHARLIE. I'm not talking to —"A vibe?"

CLEA. Oh is "vibe" like a totally uncool word, in your little tribe —

LEWIS. Hey, Nick!

CHARLIE. No no, it's got a real seventies charm that I find particularly captivating in someone who wasn't born until Nineteen eighty-two —

CLEA. Oh, I'm young, well, I guess you're not, huh, that's really the problem isn't it?

(A beat.)

LEWIS. Whoa.

CHARLIE. There's no problem, Clea. I don't know you. I came by my friend's loft — his name is Edward, by the way, and he's an actor, he's not in "the fashion industry," he's a very fine stage actor even though he's not doing seven off-Broadway shows at once —

LEWIS. Look, look, look —

CLEA. Yeah, whatever —

CHARLIE. I'm here because my friend asked me to come by, and I did that and now I'm going. Nice to meet you.

CLEA. If there isn't a problem, what are you so bent out of shape about?

CHARLIE. You're really a fucking piece of work.

LEWIS. Charlie.

CHARLIE. What? She's a fucking idiot!

LEWIS. Hey, whoa, are you —

CLEA. No. It's okay. There were, obviously, there were some things said here, that maybe rubbed you the wrong way and I am totally willing to talk about that. I mean I apologize for that. But you were like jumping all over me because I said surreal, and I just started to feel stupid. So I apologize. If I was edgy or something.

LEWIS. Look, it's okay.

CLEA. Maybe I should get some vodka or something.

CHARLIE. I thought you didn't drink.

CLEA. I don't! I mean, I really don't. Hardly ever.

LEWIS. You want me to get you a vodka?

CLEA. Would you?

LEWIS. Sure.

(He goes. After a minute, CHARLIE sighs, makes another move to desert her.)

CHARLIE. Listen, I really do have to...

CLEA. I totally understand. This is your friend's party, you should go, go, you know a ton of people here probably. You need to talk to Nick, that's clearly a big thing, or something.

CHARLIE. Nick's an asshole.

CLEA. Whatever.

CHARLIE. Look — Are you here alone?

CLEA. No! God, no, I came with a friend, I don't know where she is. She's like the total scene-machine.

CHARLIE. Can I ask — I mean — Why do you talk like that?

CLEA. *(Defensive but firm.)* I talk the way I talk. I'm not apologizing for that. I mean, I apologize for before, acting like a little edgy, but language is a totally idiosyncratic and very personal, very organic function of you know, someone's humanity, so I'm not apologizing for my language.

CHARLIE. Okay.

CLEA. Okay what?

CHARLIE. Okay nothing. That's actually a fairly coherent and legitimate point.

(LEWIS RETURNS with three drinks. He hands them around.)

CLEA. *(Continuing)* Thanks.

(She downs the drink. LEWIS and CHARLIE watch her.)

CLEA. *(Continuing)* Wow! That is... good. Ah. Wow. Mmmm.

LEWIS. *(Cautious)* Should I get you another?

CLEA. No, I just want to feel this one first. I never drink. My mother was an alcoholic so I have to be like totally careful.

LEWIS. So where are you from, Clea?

CLEA. Ohio. Isn't that hilarious? Plus I just got here, like, what, six months ago? It's a lot, I mean, to get used to. But it's so alive, just walking down the street, the energy. I'm like from, you know, the middle of nowhere, and I land here and it's so much more intense than even you think. Not like I'm some sort of cornball. But more like I'm alert, you know, really on fire with how amazing it is to be here. Because my experience, already, and don't take this personally, but people here are like not awake. To what — I don't want to sound judgmental because that is so not what I'm about but like what I mean is, I had this job interview yesterday, or the day be — no yesterday, I'm pretty sure, I had this amazing opportunity to work on this talk show, not that I think television is really a good place for anyone but I'm like trying to be open, really open, and anyway the agency sends me in to talk to this person who is like, she does something, I can't even tell what it is, for this talk show, like these people go on the television and interview movie stars or you know important people. She's the person who books, you know, she books people.

LEWIS. Really? 'Cause —

CHARLIE. Yeah, so you went in —

CLEA. Yeah, so I'm walking around this television studio, and there's like lights and you know "people" and everyone is so phony and intense, you just want to puke, like, what is supposed to be going on in a place like that? It's just like a void, with a lot of color in it. Totally bizarre. And this woman is so into it. Her name is like "Stella." And everything is just do this, be perfect.

LEWIS. Stella?

CLEA. Right? Right? And she could not be more like a Nazi priestess or something, she is so worked up over these phone lists and highlighting in blue and mint green who needs to get returned, who hasn't returned, just utter crap — oh and on top of it all, she's in the middle of one of those adoptions, she's one of those infertile women who is like adopting an abandoned baby from China and those calls go on the special list, like lists are the holy grail to this total Nazi, like the lists and the movie stars and this invisible baby in the middle of China is like, you know, life to her. And I'm like — look around you! This city is so alive and you're just like — I don't know. Wow I think that vodka just hit, I so don't drink. Do you know what I mean? About being alive, I mean?

LEWIS. Uh — you're alive, but Stella —

CLEA. Was totally not.

LEWIS. You know, I should tell you that I think I know that person

CLEA. Stella? You know like, Stella the Nazi priestess from T.V. Land? Really?

LEWIS. Yeah, I, I think I do.

CLEA. Come on. Like, that is so wild. How do you know her?

CHARLIE. I'm married to her.

(There is a pause while CLEA takes this in. Blackout.)

Scene 2

*(STELLA, CHARLIE and LEWIS, doing shots of tequila in
STELLA and CHARLIE'S apartment. They trade off the
bottle, and speak on top of each other.)*

STELLA. *(Pouring a shot.)* What did she call me? A
"Nazi priestess?"

CHARLIE. A frigid Nazi priestess —

LEWIS. Infertile. An infertile —

CHARLIE. It was "frigid."

STELLA. Stop it, god, you guys — Why didn't you tell
me about this last night?

CHARLIE. You were asleep. Did you want me to wake
you up and tell you I met some girl at a party who said you
were a frigid Nazi priestess?

LEWIS. It wasn't frigid!

STELLA. Why are you defending her?

LEWIS. I'm not! I'm just striving for a shred of accuracy
or something —

CHARLIE. Frigid.

LEWIS. Infertile.

CHARLIE. Frigid —

LEWIS. Infertile!

CHARLIE. Frigid—

STELLA. *(Overlap)* Stop it, stop it! What a bitch. I
mean, I was incredibly nice to this stupid person, I mean she
was patently stupid and I was so nice, and now I find out
she's what, offended, she's morally offended by my phone
lists and my highlighters? Everyone in New York has phone
lists, how are you supposed to remember who you have to

call back? And excuse me but having blue and green highlighters makes me a Nazi, and the fact that I don't kill Jews is
irrelevant? She sounds like a genius. She can hardly speak, as
I recall. She looks great in black and she can't speak the
English language, she'll do just fine in New York.

CHARLIE. I shouldn't have told you.

STELLA. Why shouldn't you tell me? Why didn't you
tell me when you got home, you met someone who called me
a frigid —

LEWIS. Infertile! Infertile!

STELLA. Why were you even talking to this stupid person —

CHARLIE. She was interesting, in a vapid way.

STELLA. She was a moron who looks good in black.

LEWIS. She wasn't a moron. She's pretty.

STELLA. Oh, for heaven's sake. I've had such a shitty
day. With my highlighters, me and my highlighters trying to
take over the world and buy Chinese babies for some sinister
fertility ritual. Like it's better to leave them in orphanages.
Children all over the world who need homes and if you
decide to take one in, it must be because you're some frigid
crazy workaholic bitch who wasn't woman enough to, you
know, have her own.

CHARLIE. Stop! Stella. Just stop, okay?

STELLA. Sorry. Sorry, Lewis.

LEWIS. It's okay.

STELLA. Are there chips? Maybe some chips would
cheer me up. Did you go to the grocery store?

CHARLIE. No.

STELLA. Oh, Charlie, come on — I have to work all
day, trying to take over the world with my highlighters,

couldn't you at least go to the grocery store?

    LEWIS. I'll go to the corner and get some chips.

    STELLA. Would you?

    LEWIS. Absolutely.

    STELLA. Thank you, Lewis. You are so nice to me.

    LEWIS. I'll get the chips.

(He stands grabs his coat and goes. There is a moment of silence.)

    STELLA. I had a horrible day.

    CHARLIE. I know.

    STELLA. That idiot not showing. Not your idiot. I'm moving onto my idiot. Who didn't show. All the shit I had to go through to get her to do us, six dozen white lilies in her dressing room, do you know what that many lilies smells like? It's enough to truly knock you out, like a disease, that many flowers. And I'm not even talking about all the stupid candy we had to buy. M&M's. Reece's cups. Twix. Why do these people think it's so cool to eat bad chocolate? Could someone, and I mean, I literally had to turn her fucking dressing room into a kind of physical representation of a complete psychotic break, lilies and bad chocolate and an EXERCISE MACHINE — she was only supposed to be in there for an hour and a half, and she needed her own STAIRMASTER, with the chocolate, what's the plan, to eat the mounds of chocolate, while you're ON the stairmaster? Turns out there was no plan, because — she didn't show.

    CHARLIE. You told me. A couple times.

    STELLA. I told you eight times. I'm turning into one of those people who say things over and over and then you have to tell them so kindly, yes you told me, like they've gone senile — this happened to my mother, after she turned fifty, she told the same story over and over and over again, it was so dreary — it was like oh, and now mom's gone insane, she's not just a pathetic nut, now she's a boring pathetic nut, telling the same story, over and over and over again —

CHARLIE. Stella. Have a drink.

STELLA. I'm half smashed already. That idiot didn't show. She did not show!

CHARLIE. You told me this morning she wasn't going to show. I mean, there's no real surprise here, is there? This is the fourth time —

STELLA. Yes, it is the fourth time, it is the fourth time she's fucked us and they insist that I book her anyway! And then it's my fucking fault we have a hole in the schedule. And there's not even a hole, I back us up every time with that idiot who makes the low carb pasta dishes, why do people believe that? Low carb pasta? Why do they —

CHARLIE. Stella —

STELLA. But it's so, demeaning, to put that on television, it's just demeaning. These people are all such liars. Low carb pasta? And it's pathetic, these women sitting out there, so hungry for this specific lie, you can eat pasta and still lose weight, that's like pathetic, it's not pathetic, it's sad, if you think about it too long, it is so sad all those women sitting out there in the house, their yearning for life to be just that little bit easier. It's probably one of the few things they have to look forward to, a nice plate of pasta with a little red sauce — only most of them, they don't go for the sensible red sauce, they go for the alfredo, or the carbonnara, I actually had to do a low fat carbonnara show once.

CHARLIE. I know.

STELLA. Oh God. I want to have compassion for these people, I feel bad —

CHARLIE. Stella —

STELLA. That they think this is a cool thing to do with their time, go and be the studio audience for a stupid talk show!

CHARLIE. Honey —

STELLA. Because they think it means something, to be on television — Only you weren't, really, you just sat there while someone else got to be on television. It's so sad. It's so so sad.

CHARLIE. No more tequila for you.

STELLA. I'm fine.

CHARLIE. Well, I'm suicidal.

STELLA. But I don't really feel sorry for them.

CHARLIE. You shouldn't!

STELLA. Oh my God of course I should. These are people who deserve compassion, these fat people who feel terrible about themselves because we're the ones, we're constantly putting on television show things like low-fat Carbonnara, low-fat foie gras, like this is some kind of good idea, to rip the pleasure and essence out of everything, that's how horrible it is to be fat. I mean these people didn't ask to be fat! And they're just surrounded by a culture — everything, everything — tells them they're worthless because they're fat! If that's not worthy of compassion, what is?

CHARLIE. Stupid people are destroying this planet. I don't have to have compassion for that.

STELLA. Low-fat foie gras. You know that's coming. That's just, out there somewhere, someone's going to try to stuff some poor duck full of low-fat corn, and tofu. You just know it.

(CHARLIE laughs. STELLA laughs. He kisses her.)

    CHARLIE. You need to take a day off.
    STELLA. Oh, God, you think?

(They continue kissing. It starts to heat up. CHARLIE tries to take off STELLA'S shirt. Laughing, she pushes him away.)

    STELLA. *(Continuing)* Stop it, Charlie! Lewis is going to come back any minute. Good heavens.
    CHARLIE. What did you say? "Good heavens?"
    STELLA. I said let go of my shirt!
    CHARLIE. I'm sure Lewis would love to see you without your shirt on —
    STELLA. Oh my god. No more tequila for you.

(She takes the bottle from him.)

    CHARLIE. You should have come to that party with us last night. I mean, it was horrible, and boring and a complete waste of time, there was no one to talk to other than a bunch of feckless drunks and this idiot girl, plus everyone was about fifteen years younger than me, so I felt like a freak —
    STELLA. Yes, I should have come, it sounds terrific.
    CHARLIE. I know! It's ridiculous. But rich people's apartments are so strangely comforting. This guy Edward's hooked up with is some sort of gazillionaire, this place is

freakishly opulent. Heated tiles in the bathroom, a fucking Picasso on the wall. Not a good one, but it was a real Picasso, why is it that real art makes real people feal phoney? Real clothes, too. This guy knows how to dress. Edward's taken to wearing silk.

STELLA. Edward?

CHARLIE Right? It looked good on him. He looked good. He looked rich. The whole place was so, we were so high up. I mean, really, in the stars. I love that about New York, when you get to go to one of those parties way above the rest of the city, there's something so surreal about it. Not surreal. Oh God. I did not mean surreal.

STELLA. It actually does sound kind of surreal.

CHARLIE. No no. No. Let's be precise. What's surreal, if anything, is one's internal state in a situation like that. Everyone acts like surreal is some sort of definition, an image can be surreal, water or or or air, how can that be surreal? Water and air, that's the definition of real. Surreal is more the connection. Or not.

STELLA. What are you talking about?

CHARLIE. *(Laughing at himself.)* I have nooo idea.

STELLA. So, did you talk to Nick?

CHARLIE. I haven't been to a party like that since I did that sitcom. Remember, when we were stuck out in L.A., and we had to keep going to all those parties in the hills —

STELLA. Those parties were hideous. You hated those parties.

CHARLIE. The food was great at those parties. And the flowers, also great, and the pools —

STELLA. All those people constantly sucking up —

CHARLIE. But they were sucking up to me.

STELLA. Oh my god. You hated every second of that —

CHARLIE. I did not hate everything.

STELLA. So tell me what Nick said.

CHARLIE. You know what we should do, Stell? We should take a trip. We should blow out the bank account and go somewhere great, Paris, or Saint Petersburg, Florence, stay at the Four Seasons, eat incredible food, wallow in bed, buy you expensive earrings, drink wine on some gorgeous town square somewhere —

STELLA. What's the matter, Charlie?

CHARLIE. Nothing's the matter! People take vacations, Stell. Come on. It would be so great to get out of this place for just a week. It would just be fun. Couldn't you use a little fun? Not thinking about all those lunatics for a whole week. Una Settamana a Firenze. A week in Florence. The Uffizi. Wine on the Piazza.

STELLA. Stop it.

CHARLIE. I'm not going to stop it. The Medici Chapel.

STELLA. Charlie, we can't just —

CHARLIE. Sure we can. We could go for two weeks. Possiamo andareper due settimane Leather gloves. Gorgeous earrings. Joilli, sono mola costosi Botticelli.

STELLA. *(Laughing)* This is not — it's just not —

CHARLIE. Yes it is. It is. Say yes. Say yes. Say "si". Say, "si, Charlie…"

(He starts to kiss her. She laughs and kisses him back. It starts to heat up. LEWIS calls from the hallway.)

LEWIS. *(Calling)* Can I come back now?

CHARLIE. Vada Via! Go away!

STELLA. Charlie...

CHARLIE. Go away! Go away!

STELLA. It's fine, I'm done melting down. I need some food, I have to eat something.

(She stands, goes to the door and opens it. LEWIS brings in chips.)

LEWIS. I didn't know what kind. They had all these different flavor nachos. Like, fake guacamole and fake ranch, and fake chili something, fake onion something...

(He hands them all out.)

STELLA. Oh God this is so nice, and horrifying at the same time. You are so nice to just buy all these chips for me.

(She smiles at him.)

CHARLIE. I'm starving. We should order something real.

STELLA. *(Eating chips.)* So did Nick even show up at Ed's stupid party?

LEWIS. Yeah, he was there.

STELLA. Nick was there? So what did he say, how did it go?

CHARLIE. *(Slight beat.)* I didn't talk to him.

STELLA. What?

CHARLIE. I didn't get a chance.

STELLA. You didn't talk to him?

CHARLIE. I didn't stay that long.

STELLA. But that's why you went.

CHARLIE. I wasn't in the right mood.

STELLA. What kind of "mood" do you have to be in to —

CHARLIE. Oh for God's sake —

STELLA. Oh for God's sake, what? *(Beat)* Charlie?

CHARLIE. I didn't talk to him. I didn't want to talk to him, so I didn't talk to him.

STELLA. Well, that's just brilliant.

LEWIS. Are you hungry? Maybe I should get some like real food.

STELLA. Yeah maybe you should.

CHARLIE. No, don't go, you don't have to —

STELLA. Yes, go, Lewis —

CHARLIE. We're not getting into this.

STELLA. We're not?

LEWIS. It wasn't the right moment, Stella, it really wasn't. Nick was like surrounded by all these people and to even get to him was just —

CHARLIE. *(To LEWIS.)* Do not excuse me to my own wife!

STELLA. Well that's really nice.

CHARLIE. We are not talking about this, Stella!

STELLA. You can tell me about the person who called me a frigid Nazi priestess but you can't —

CHARLIE. There's nothing to tell. He showed up. I was in a bad mood, so I didn't talk to him.

STELLA. Well then you have to call him —

CHARLIE. I'm not calling Nick —

STELLA. He's got a pilot, Charlie —

CHARLIE. I know all about that, Stella. You've told me about —

STELLA. Oh don't do that —

LEWIS. Listen, you guys, maybe—

STELLA. He loves you. You have to remind him —

CHARLIE. Nick does not —

STELLA. You went to high school with him! You were best friends for —

CHARLIE. Oh my god. We were never, ever —

STELLA. Yes you were and you're a terrific actor, he knows how good you are, he knew you when you were —

CHARLIE. *(Bitter)* When I was working?

STELLA. *(Unflinching)* Yes. When you were working. A lot. You're a wonderful actor, Charlie, come in, you have to fight for yourself —

CHARLIE. Talking to Nick at a party is not going to get him to give me a part in his pilot!

STELLA. Well, if you don't talk to him he's certainly not going to give you a part, I can guarantee you —

CHARLIE. Oh yeah he really is desperate to have people he knew in a previous life suck up to him at parties —

STELLA. *(Firm)* People like that, Charlie. These people, these T.V. people like it when you suck up — they like it —

CHARLIE. Oh. That's why I should do it —

STELLA. You should do it because you need a fucking job —

CHARLIE. *(Overlap)* Because sucking up to assholes so that you can work in television is clearly something that's worked out so well for you —

STELLA. It's certainly worked out well for you, since I pay all the bills around here.

(Beat.)

LEWIS. You guys want some chips? These Cool Ranch chips are surprisingly...

CHARLIE. Shut up, Lewis!

STELLA. Could you please stop taking this out on Lewis? He is not the problem here.

CHARLIE. I'm well aware.

STELLA. *(Beat, then.)* Nick —

CHARLIE. *(Strained)* Nick doesn't have a pilot. They just say that, people run around this fucking city saying things like "he has a pilot," "he has a go picture" "it's got a greenlight," when it's all just crap, it's just not even, it's lying taken to it's natural conclusion, these people are lying to make themselves feel better and they don't even know that they're lying and then everybody else around starts to tell the same lie and it's never true. That's the fucking punchline. Everybody's running around like psychotic sheep, bleating, "He has a pilot! He has a pilot —"

STELLA. He does have a pilot.

CHARLIE. Oh, God —

STELLA. You need a job!

CHARLIE. I know I need a job!

STELLA. Why would it kill you —

CHARLIE. I don't know, Stella!

STELLA. You just have to talk to him at a party —

CHARLIE. *(Furious)* I am not talking to Nick! I'm not talking to that asshole! Do you understand me? I am not talking to Nick.

(He goes. STELLA and LEWIS look at each other, stunned. Blackout.)

Scene 3

(CLEA and LEWIS, in LEWIS'S apartment. There is a cheese plate on a table.)

LEWIS. Can I get you a drink? Vodka, you're a vodka girl, right?

CLEA. Water would be fantastic. Just a glass of water. I really don't drink.

LEWIS. Oh I know, I just, at Edward's party the other night you were like, you know —

CLEA. I was not drunk. At all. I hope you don't think that. Because I totally —

LEWIS. No no. I just meant you had one or two, so I thought that "no drinking" thing was not like a hard and fast rule or anything.

CLEA. *(Indignant)* Is this a problem for you? Is it like important to you that I drink? Because that is so not something I feel comfortable with.

LEWIS. *(Alarmed)* No! Oh my God of course not!

CLEA. I mean I asked for a glass of water and you're turning this into some major moral crisis here.

LEWIS. No —

CLEA. And I completely object to being called a "Vodka Girl." I mean, I told you before, my mother is an alcoholic so it's just not something I can be casual about, and for you to like insinuate, whatever, that I was drunk or something at that party —

LEWIS. No no, that's not what I meant at all. It's just, when you said "water," I just — it doesn't seem...

CLEA. Doesn't seem what, like you could get me drunk

on water? Do you find like, drunk women attractive?

LEWIS. *(Sad)* I was just, no! — I was just going to say that water doesn't seem festive. It seems so plain. I know everybody drinks it now, out of bottles and everything, but it just always to me it just seems so — plain.

CLEA. Plain is good. Plain is strong. Water is the strength of the earth. I don't find that "plain." I find that inspiring.

LEWIS. I know. I know! *(Beat)* Let me get you a glass of water.

(He goes, to get her water.)

CLEA. Wait a minute. I'm sorry. I'm sorry, I'm a little, reactive. You're right, I said I'd come over for a drink and water, it's just not nice or something, I apologize. I know you're trying to be real nice and I'd love a vodka. I had a real ridiculous day, vodka is actually an excellent idea. Maybe put some ice in it.

LEWIS. Okay.

(He goes off. She looks around the apartment, calls after him.)

CLEA. So. How's your friend the Nazi priestess?

LEWIS. *(Calling back.)* Oh, she's, you know, she's really not that bad.

(LEWIS re-enters with a glass of vodka, and ice. He hands it to her, pours her a drink.)

CLEA. I know! I feel so terrible, I was totally exaggerating that interview I had and the whole thing was like, you know, just the sort of thing you say when you're not thinking!

LEWIS. Well, you didn't know —

CLEA. *(Sparkling now.)* No, but your friend did! And he just let me keep going! It was just like a little hostile, you know. To let me go on like that. I was like, ouch! Got a little problem in the sack with the old wife, maybe?

LEWIS. No, no — not at all — they're really tight, they've been together —

CLEA. Oh totally, I didn't mean —

LEWIS. Forever! Fourteen years or something. And they're adopting this baby. They're great.

CLEA. Hey, what do I know. *(She downs her drink.)* Oh. Wow. Mmm. That is so — wow.

LEWIS. *(Disturbed now.)* He was just tense, that night. About other stuff.

CLEA. Look — don't treat me like I'm stupid. I mean, I think I know the difference between tension and hostility. So it's not like I'm stupid.

LEWIS. I don't think you're stupid!

CLEA. Well, you're acting kind of —

LEWIS. No, no —

CLEA. Because I really object to that. A lot of people treat me like I'm some sort of flake because I look a certain way, and that is just, I don't want to sound like some hideous feminist, but I will not be treated like a stupid person. I want to be clear on that.

LEWIS. God, no! I wouldn't have asked you to come over, if I thought —

CLEA. Well, good. Because I respect what you are saying, but I'm just, you know, your friend has like a lot of angry energy. Which I like! I mean, it's not like I'm saying that's a bad thing, if he's married to a screaming woman who is like obsessed with phone lists and highlighters —

LEWIS. She's really nice —

CLEA. Oh totally. I so totally get that. I'm just saying. I don't judge him if he's hostile about it.

(There is an awkward pause.)

LEWIS. I'm gonna get myself a drink. Can I refresh that for you? You know what, I'm just going to bring the bottle.

(He goes. CLEA considers the cheese plate for a moment. LEWIS RE-ENTERS, pouring himself a stiff drink, and watches her.)

LEWIS. *(Continuing)* Would you like a piece of cheese, or —

CLEA. Oh God no. I am totally on a diet. Food is like disgusting to me.

LEWIS. It is?

CLEA. Oh my God, are you kidding? Most of the things people put in their mouths are like totally just like eating death. That's how bad our food is for us. Do you not know this? They proved, somebody proved that eating is killing people. And that if you eat like hardly anything? Just like lettuce and maybe a few vegetables or something, everyday, that could make you live to be like a hundred and fifty years old. This is true, I read about it in The New York Times.

LEWIS. Eating —

CLEA. Is terrible for you. Don't do it.

LEWIS. Wow.

CLEA. Isn't it?

LEWIS. Yeah, that's —'cause everything I've heard before this, you know, food is considered to be life-sustaining.

CLEA. Well, except didn't you suspect that it was probably bad for you? All those people getting fat, all over America, just like buying food from grocery stores or going into restaurants where they give you these portions, and everything has chemicals in it, or who knows what, who knows what they put in our food anymore.

LEWIS. Wow. Not eating makes you live forever. Who, uh, knew.

CLEA. Well, I know it sounds weird but...*(Suddenly spooked.)* You know what? Forget it. I'm sorry. This is, I should go —

LEWIS. No! Why?

CLEA. I don't feel right, this just doesn't feel right.

LEWIS. Come on, you just got here! Have another drink —

CLEA. I don't really drink. I'm feeling embarrassed now, that I have to keep telling you that.

LEWIS. Please. I really like you. I, I want you to stay. Please.

CLEA. You just want to sleep with me.

LEWIS. What — that is — no!

CLEA. You don't want to sleep with me?

LEWIS. I didn't say that —

CLEA. See? This just happens to me all the time. Just, everyone just wants to sleep with me. Every guy I meet, it's just, I don't know what to do about it — because I am like, a very sensitive person —

LEWIS. I didn't just — invite you over here for sex, if that's what you think —

CLEA. It is what I think! It is!

LEWIS. No, no. No, no no — no —

CLEA. Oh, please —

LEWIS. No! I really like you. I think you're really interesting. I do.

CLEA. It's just, everybody just falls in love with me all the time. So many guys are just obsessed, and I — I mean, I'm just overwhelmed. I'm from Ohio, it's different there. I feel very out of control here.

(There is a long pause while LEWIS tries to figure out what to do next.)

LEWIS. Would you like a glass of water, or something?

CLEA. Maybe some vodka, I don't know. I'm kind of tense.

(He nods, and pours her a drink. He hands it to her. She holds it.)

LEWIS. Here, sit down. Come on, sit down.

CLEA. It's just been a very confusing day.

LEWIS. What happened?

CLEA. I don't want to talk about it.

LEWIS. *(Nice)* Come on. I'm interested.

CLEA. *(Sudden)* Would you like to kiss me?

LEWIS. *(A beat.)* Is this a trick question?

CLEA. You just, you seem like a really nice person, and I would really like it. If you would kiss me. If you're interested.

LEWIS. Yes, I'm interested! But I don't want to — you know —

CLEA. Do you think I'm a freak, or something? Because I've been freaking out here?

LEWIS. No, you just said that you were overwhelmed by men showing too much sexual interest in you, so I —

CLEA. I know, I know, I did just say that. But I would really like it if you would kiss me. I just think it might make me feel better, or — forget it —

LEWIS. No! No. No! It's okay. Really.

(He sets his drink down, takes her's from her, sets it down, leans in carefully and kisses her.)

LEWIS. *(Continuing)* How's that?
CLEA. It's nice.

(She kisses him again. They start making out. There is a knock at the door. They ignore it for a while, but the knocking continues.)

LEWIS. Go away!
CHARLIE. Hey Lewis! You in there?
CLEA. Oh my god, is that your friend?
CHARLIE. Come on, you got to let me in, man —
LEWIS. Go away, Charlie —

(She pushes away from him.)

CLEA. No, it's fine, it's fine — you have to let him in, please, he's your friend! I'm fine! Let him in.

(LEWIS goes to the door, and opens it. CHARLIE ENTERS, carrying a script.)

CHARLIE. I saw that shithead Nick. I went and had fucking lunch with that fucking shithead.

(He sees CLEA.)

CLEA. Hi.
CHARLIE. Oh. Hi!

(He is not happy to see her.)

LEWIS. Clea just came over for a —

(LEWIS tips his head toward the open door, indicating that he would like CHARLIE to leave. CHARLIE railroads over him, not noticing.)

CHARLIE. That fuckhead. I said, did I not say, he is a fuck-head? I told her that this would be a waste of my fucking time. I told everyone. Did I not? Did I not? What is this, vodka?

(He picks it up and uncorks it, then proceeds to drink from the bottle as he rants.)

CHARLIE. *(Continuing)* Because he is a fuck. You know this to be true. I mean, in high school he was a fuck, and in college, he was a fuck, and time is not a friend to people like that. I mean, it's not like they mellow. It's not like they ripen, like a good bottle of wine! No no no, Nick is still Nick, only

more so. And now someone has actually told him that they
are going to make his fucking pilot, which was just what Nick
needed to really put the final touches on his complete lack of
character! Give him a shred of power over hopeless and desperate people, that'll really make him shine! Not that I even
believe it. I don't give a shit how many people say it. I do not
believe that they are going to make his fucking pilot! Which
by the way, he gave to me, to read, so on the sidewalk, out-
side the restaurant, after our cappuccinos, he took off and I
opened it up and I read it, and I'm sure you'll be stunned to
hear that it is utter mindless, soulless, uninspired, unoriginal,
bereft, soul-sucking crap. Which is the only thing that makes
me think he might actually be telling the truth. The fact that
his fucking pilot is so irredeemably awful, such a complete
expression of the bankruptcy of the American character, that
alone argues for the shred of a possibility that he is flirting
with the truth for once in his life, with his assertion that they
are going to make his astonishingly shitty pilot. It is so bad,
there actually is a possibility that they're going to make it.
Against all my better judgment, I truly have to concede that.
    CLEA. Wow.
    CHARLIE. Oh you have no idea. This is the tip of the
iceberg. This day was, I actually had lunch with that asshole
at a place called "Grind". "Grind." Next thing you know
they're going to be calling restaurants things like "Hot"
"Wet" "Fuck me," someday we are all going to be forced to
have lunch with assholes at some restaurant called "Fuck
me." Nick of course is on his cell phone for a full five minutes before he can even say hello. Five minutes of the finger
in the air, twitching — *(He sticks his finger in the air, twitch-
es it.)* While I sit there grinning, like a SCHMUCK, it's

okay, man, I know you got to hang on this endless phone call 'cause you're so fucking important, you're a completely essential piece of the whole mind-numbing motor that keeps capitalism itself running, you're the guy, you're the guy, and I'm just some stupid SHITHEAD who needs to lick your ass —

LEWIS. Hey, Charlie —

CHARLIE. C'mon I'm not making this up! I'm not even exaggerating! It was like a scene out of some bad Nineteenth Century novel, or a good one, even, War and Peace, he's Prince Somebody and I'm the bastard son of Somebody Else, who remembers, except for the licking of the ass part. Except if we were in Russia, in the Nineteenth Century, there would be a form for it all, a ritual, a way to keep your dignity while you said, please your highness, save my fucking worthless piece of shit self. Give me some money. I'm fucking broke, I'm not a man, GIVE ME SOME MONEY. And if you do, I will go to Siberia for you, I will face Bonaparte with my bare hands, I will fling myself into the abyss, just give me some fucking money so that I don't have to — Plus he's thin! Did I tell you this? You remember Nick, he was just like a normal guy, right? Aside from being a fuck? He's lost like forty pounds. And I mean, he was normal, before, it's not like he was fat, he was just normal so now he's like — it's like his face is just sitting right on his skull. You're like talking to a really skinny skull version of who Nick used to be. And he's dressed all in black, this bizarre black suit with a black silk t shirt under it, so he actually does look like one of those freaks from a vampire movie, do they honestly think that looks good, in Hollywood? They must! I don't know. I don't know. So then he orders like a huge slab of red meat, because that's all he can eat, apparently. That's how he got so thin, by eat-

ing only raw meat. I swear to you, I am not making ONE
WORD of this up. And I'm completely, I am just trying to
stay focused on the sucking up end of the conversation, trying not say anything truthful, just stay in the conversation, let
him know that I'm a total failure of a human being, but I also
know and appreciate that fact that he is not.

LEWIS. Charlie —

CHARLIE. Oh, stop it, don't even, that is completely
what. those conversations are about! That is what they are
about! And I'm doing it, I am absolutely humiliating myself
so that I can get Nick to give me an audition for a teeny tiny
part in a pilot I don't even believe exists, when he looks at my
plate and says, "I could never eat that. That is just too rich."
I mean, he's got a slab of red meat the size of Nebraska sitting on his plate, and I've got a plate of mushroom puree, sitting in front of me. Mushroom puree, with about five or six
itty bitty scallops on top of it, I got so fucking self-conscious
about how fucking thin he was, that I ordered a completely
girly meal, scallops in mushroom puree, just so I wouldn't
have to think about that crap while I castrated myself for this
— this — skull-person — and then he — he — *(He stops
himself. Sits. Takes a big hit off the vodka bottle.)* Sorry.
Forget about it. I don't even know what I'm saying.

CLEA. No. Are you kidding? That was incredible. What
you just said. That was — wow. I'm like tingling.

CHARLIE. Oh, good. *(Then)* Am I interrupting?

CLEA. No!

LEWIS. Well, kind of —

CHARLIE. Oh, shit —

CLEA. No, it's fine —

CHARLIE. You're, like, having a drink here —

LEWIS. Yes.

CHARLIE. I'm sorry. I'll take off.

CLEA. God no, that was horrible what you just went through! You have to stay with your friends and just like, at least stay, and and and stay, until you feel like a human being again!

CHARLIE. Thanks, but —

CLEA. *(To Lewis.)* He should stay, right? You can't send him back to the Nazi priestess at least until he just relaxes or —

LEWIS. She's really not that bad —

CHARLIE. No, she's great. She's great.

CLEA. Oh I know. I totally know. But come on. Should I get you a glass? So that you don't have to keep —

(She gestures, drinking from the bottle.)

CHARLIE. Maybe that's a good idea.

CLEA. Totally. They're like in here, right? I'll get another glass.

(She goes. There is a long moment of silence. CHARLIE tries hard not to laugh. LEWIS looks at him, not amused.)

CHARLIE. *(Laughing at this.)* You said you asked her for drinks, I didn't know that meant today.

LEWIS. Yes! Today! Today!

CHARLIE. Come on, you're not actually getting anywhere are you?

LEWIS. Yes, I am, I was, at least, I don't seem to be anymore —

CHARLIE. She's a fucking moron, Lewis —

LEWIS. I don't care!

CHARLIE. You want me to take off?

LEWIS. Yes! No. I don't — she's very — sensitive. If you left, I don't think — I don't know —

CHARLIE. I'm sorry, man —

CLEA. *(Re-entering)* What are you sorry about?

(She takes the vodka bottle from CHARLIE and pours him a drink.)

CHARLIE. Just about coming over here and losing it.

CLEA. Don't apologize! Are you kidding! You are so in touch with your feelings.

CHARLIE. That's not actually something you want to say to a guy, to make him feel better. That's not actually considered a compliment, on our planet.

CLEA. Well, you are so just wrong about that. Because if you lose, like, knowing who you are? If you lose that? You're lost. And then the bastards like Nick, they just rule the world.

CHARLIE. They already rule the world, Clea.

CLEA. They don't rule you.

(She hands him his drink.)

CHARLIE. Yeah, uh, thanks.

CLEA. Besides, it's so great you came by because I totally need to apologize. That stuff I said the other night? I mean, whoa. My bad, my total bad.

CHARLIE. It's okay.

CLEA. That's very very decent of you to say. Because I felt terrible afterwards, I was being so rude about everybody.

Especially your wife! The things I said! Here —

(She pours him more vodka.)

CHARLIE. Look, forget it, would you? We all say shitty things about people we don't know. It's the only true pleasure left in the world, trashing other people. Especially when they have something you want: Money. Or power. Or just, coherence —

LEWIS. Hey, Charlie maybe we should —

CHARLIE. *(Complete overlap, revving again.)* Not that I think Nick is coherent in any way, any larger cosmic truth has evaded Nick altogether —

LEWIS. Yeah, but I just don't know that —

CHARLIE. *(Complete overlap.)* But he's still the object of desire, isn't he? Him and that fucking pilot. He could be shooting kiddie porn as far as anyone's concerned and I still have to suck up, don't I, that's how degraded this whole fucking planet has gotten, SUCK UP to assholes like Nick because they have something you must want even though you don't, you don't want it, everyone just thinks, God, it's like we don't even know how to have a real DESIRE anymore! It's all the opposite of enlightenment, remember when that was a goal? Nowadays if someone said to you, what you want out of life? And you said, I don't know, enlightenment, what do you think would happen? WHAT DO YOU THINK WOULD HAPPEN? These are the fucking end times. The entire fucking culture has devolved to such a point that what we WANT, what we DESIRE isn't love or passion or sex or money, it's MEANINGLESSNESS. And that's what I'm supposed to sell myself for. Time to sell it, my heart, my soul, my common sense, my hope, my dreams, my pride, anything that means anything at all to my little pre-conscious, sub-conscious self, all of it goes on the auction block for what? That's what I want to know. What am I supposed to get? To give up everything? What do I get? *(Beat)* I have a feeling we're gonna need more vodka. You got another bottle back there?

LEWIS. Sorry.

CLEA. Can you, can you go get some?

LEWIS. Oh —

CHARLIE. No, no — God, I'm sorry — I got to get out of here, I'm just —

CLEA. No no please. Don't be ridiculous. I'll go —

LEWIS & CHARLIE, No — no — no —

(Beat.)

CLEA. Just I mean, for vodka.

CHARLIE. I'll go, it's fine. Really. There's a liquor store just a couple blocks, besides, I'm the one sucking it down.

CLEA. You're in crisis! You just got here, and you're wrecked! Lewis, can you go?

(Beat.)

LEWIS. Maybe we should go to dinner.

CLEA. All three of us? Do you want to?

CHARLIE. *(Slight beat.)* You know what? I'm going to take off — I really —

CLEA. Stop it! That is insane. Besides, I totally want to hear about all of this. I mean, you have no idea how inspiring it is to hear you just talk! To someone like me? Because I am so new here, I mean, I just came like minutes ago from Ohio and the whole world seems so — just insane, you know — I am so confused like all the time — and then I listen to you, and I know I'm not crazy. *(To LEWIS, gushing.)* Doesn't he make you feel like that? Just less crazy?

CHARLIE. Actually, Clea, I am being alarmingly self-indulgent, and I need to go home.

CLEA. If you wanted to go home, wouldn't you have been there by now? And you are not being self-indulgent. I think it's sad that you think that. Because you're like on fire. They don't deserve you.

LEWIS. They, who?

CLEA. None of them.

LEWIS. Maybe we could all go. For the booze, I mean.

CLEA. Do you need money?

LEWIS. No!

CHARLIE. That's a good idea, we'll all go.

CLEA. But that doesn't make any sense. Besides, you must be starving! All you had for lunch was a couple of scallops and some mushrooms. Aren't you hungry?

CHARLIE. Yeah, but —

CLEA. *(To LEWIS.)* Could you pick up some pizza, too? There's like a stand down there someplace, right?

LEWIS. I thought you only ate vegetables.

CLEA. Not for me! I can't eat a thing, I am so totally bloated right now. But I would have another drink. I mean, I don't drink, I really don't? But sometimes it clearly is just what has to happen. It'll only take you like a minute, right?

LEWIS. Yeah. *(Beat)* Yes! Sure!

CLEA. Great!

LEWIS. Yeah, okay. I'll be right back.

(He grabs his jacket and goes to the door, where he turns and looks at them.)

LEWIS. *(Continuing)* I'll — be right back!

(He goes, shutting the door behind him. CLEA turns to CHARLIE, smiling.)

CLEA. That is incredible, the way you define things with so much fire. I really can't even, I mean, it's totally overwhelming.
CHARLIE. Yeah.

(He smiles at her, brief, looks away, at the cheese plate, then stands, moves away from her.)

CLEA. You knew I was going to be here, didn't you?
CHARLIE. What? No.
CLEA. I could tell. When you walked in.
CHARLIE. No, that's —
CLEA. You're lying.
CHARLIE. You know what? I'm taking off.
CLEA. That's not what you want to do.
CHARLIE. Actually, it is. Just tell Lewis — you don't have to tell him anything, he will be so relieved I'm gone, he won't care.

(He heads for the door.)

CLEA. You spent the whole day doing things that made you feel shitty about yourself. Why don't you just do something you want to do?

(She gets close to him. He takes a step back.)

CHARLIE. You're on a date with my best friend.

CLEA. So?

CHARLIE. So I think I'd like to pretend that I still have a shred of integrity —

CLEA. Why?

CHARLIE. Because — you know — because I don't have much else left.

CLEA. You don't know what you have. Because nobody has been telling you. They've just been telling you what you're not. Why don't you try being what you are?

(She starts to kiss him. He pushes her away for a moment. Then, he leans in and kisses her, pushing her back to the couch. They land on the couch and start to make out in earnest. Blackout.)

ACT II

Scene 4

(CHARLIE'S apartment. CLEA and CHARLIE are having sex on the couch, and elsewhere. They are both in a half state of undress, as if they hit the ground running. It is quite athletic. After an extended and quite vocal climax, they collapse.)

CLEA. Oh, God. Don't stop. No, don't stop. Don't stop!
CHARLIE. You got to give me a minute here, Clea.
CLEA. No, don't stop —
CHARLIE. How old did you say you were?

(He means it half as a joke, but it does stop her.)

CLEA. No no don't do that. Don't categorize me.

CHARLIE. *(Still breathless.)* Asking you how old you are is categorizing?

CLEA You're trying to define age as a life characteristic. As like, something that says something about a person.

45

CHARLIE. It does say, how old you are.

CLEA. No, it doesn't. It really doesn't. You say, "how old are you" like I'm young and you're old, like that's some joke, because you think you're old? But you're timeless. You're like this incredible lion who's been stalking the earth since the dawn of nature, or something.

CHARLIE.Tell me, do you actually believe all this crap that you keep spouting?

CLEA. Of course I believe it. Maybe you should try believing it, too. Why wouldn't you want to believe that you're a timeless lion? Isn't that better than thinking you're some old loser who can't get a job?

(She climbs on him and starts to kiss him. He pushes her away, sudden, stands and puts his pants on.)

CLEA. *(Continuing)* No no. Don't do that. That's what I'm saying, that's not who you are!

CHARLIE. We have to get you out of here.

(He starts to dress, and straighten out the room again.)

CLEA. We just got here.

CHARLIE. And now we have to go.

CLEA. You said she was going to be at work, all afternoon, she's off screaming somewhere, come on, you said, we have all afternoon. Be a lion.

CHARLIE. I think we've had enough of the lion, Clea.

CLEA. I haven't. I mean it. I can go all day, and all night, I could go a whole weekend. Have you ever done that? Just, spent a whole weekend inside, doing things...

CHARLIE. Don't you get sore?

CLEA. You want to find out?

CHARLIE. Jesus! You're like, it's like talking to a porno movie —

CLEA. You are so hung up about the way I talk all the time!

CHARLIE. Well, it's very unusual, Clea, to find someone so remarkably uninhibited in so many ways —

CLEA. Yeah but you always turn it around, like you don't like it. You make it sound like it's maybe not so great, the way I am. That I'm sort of stupid, or just stupid or something —

CHARLIE. "Voracious" is actually the word I was thinking of.

CLEA. Yeah, like that's a bad thing. But you know what? You like it. It's actually driving you crazy how much you like it. Why can't you just say it? If I'm voracious then you're something that wants voracious more than anything it ever saw before.

CHARLIE. How can you know so much and so little at the same time?

CLEA. You have no idea, how much I know. Come on. You said we have all afternoon.

(She kisses him. He is increasingly a lost man. He tries to push her away.)

CHARLIE. We do have all afternoon. Just, not here.

CLEA. Ohhh please...

CHARLIE. Listen to me. This is my apartment.

CLEA. I know. I love it that you brought me here. It's so hostile.

CHARLIE. You are really something.

CLEA. Yes, I am. And you're the one who brought me here, to have sex in your apartment.

CHARLIE. Stella could just walk in on us —

CLEA. *(Laughing)* That would be hilarious.

CHARLIE. Yeah, no, it wouldn't.

(He pushes her away, firm. Looks at her, suddenly simple and clear and a little desperate.)

CHARLIE. *(Continuing)* I mean, you understand what this is. We're clear on what this is, right?

CLEA. Relax. I know what this is. You're at a place, so am I. This is that place.

CHARLIE. Yes.

CLEA. It's what you need and I want, and that's why it's so hot. Trust me. I understand what this is.

CHARLIE. Good.

(Unsure, hoping that was clear, he leaves the room. She watches him go, goes to her purse, and takes out an apple, starts to eat, and call to him in the next room.)

CLEA. *(Yelling)* You know what we should do tonight? My friend can get me into this party. It's up on the upper west side so it is totally not like a really hip scene or anything, but there's going to be some movie stars there, she wouldn't tell me who, but they also have this hot tub there? On the roof. She went to a party at this place a couple weeks ago, and everyone takes their clothes off and gets in the hot tub. And then they have these cater waiters come around, I'm not kidding, with sushi. So you sit in the hot tub and like talk and eat sushi naked. It sounds so nineties, doesn't it? Movie stars and sushi in a hot tub? Maybe they'll play R.E.M. on the "record player." Or do lines of cocaine. It's so unbelievably retro, a hot tub on the roof. I soo want to go.

CHARLIE. *(ENTERING)* I've been to this party.

CLEA. Get out.

CHARLIE. I swear to god, I went to that party twenty years ago. Riverside Drive, ninety-six or seven and Riverside.

CLEA. I don't know.

CHARLIE. Sushi and cocaine in the hot tub on the roof? I went to that party. No kidding. I was doing this play off Broadway, and one of the other actors knew somebody who was going to this party, on the upper west side. This rich guy, nobody knew his name, and the place is like a mansion, right, he owns the whole building and it's got art deco everything, completely tasteless. The place was huge, like five floors, people screwing in corners of the den and the living room, there was a three way going on in one room, I'm not kidding, real hedonistic shit. And then there's that the hot tub up there on the roof with the greenhouse. *(Laughing now.)* He's got a fucking greenhouse up there, growing cactuses and hibiscus, something, I can't believe I remember this, everybody was completely coked out of their minds, like all night, till five, six in the morning. That's how stupid we all were. It's amazing most of us are still alive. I was such hot shit. That play was unintelligible but I got amazing reviews, and I was...the world was on fire for me, boy. Sushi and cocaine and whatever I wanted. God that was fun. That was really fun.

CLEA. Well, guess what, it's your lucky night. Because

you can go to that party again. With me.

CHARLIE. *(Reality check.)* I can't go to a party with you.

CLEA. Why not?

CHARLIE. Because I can't.

CLEA. It'll be realllly fun. That's what you said, it was reallly fun.

CHARLIE. I'm not going to a party with you, Clea!

CLEA. No one will see us! That's the whole point, that scene is completely over, so it won't matter!

CHARLIE. Great.

CLEA. You said yourself, the guy who owns this place is so nobody on earth that is important, just some rich guy with a lot of money and a house with a hot tub, we can totally just go together. I mean, with my friend, we can dump her when we get there, which will be fine with her, she dumps me all the time.

CHARLIE. Look, I have — a life, Clea.

CLEA. Don't you mean, a "wife?"

CHARLIE. Yeah. That's what I mean. And like you said that scene is over. I'm not going to a party with you.

(He continues straightening the apartment.)

CLEA. No, come on, forget about her! You should see how much happier you are when you forget about her. We don't have to go to any party. Let's just pretend we're at a party. We're in the hot tub right now. No. No. Let's skip the hot tub. I like the sound of those rooms, where people are just doing things, in the middle of somebody's house, who they don't even know whose house it is. Let's just think about doing it in front of everybody, in somebody else's room....

(She reaches up and kisses him. He kisses her back. As things are heating up again, the door opens. STELLA ENTERS, and sees them. She stops. After a moment, she speaks.)

STELLA. Charlie. I'm here.

(This is the first CHARLIE and CLEA are aware of her entrance.)

CHARLIE. Shit.
CHARLIE. Stella.
STELLA. What are you doing, Charlie?
CHARLIE. Nothing. No — this isn't —
STELLA. What, what it looks like? It isn't what it looks like?
CHARLIE. Stella—
STELLA. In my home? You brought, to my home?

(CLEA starts to laugh, embarrassed. She tries to stop herself, but simply can't.)

CLEA. I'm sorry. Oh, I am so sorry. But this is just hideous. Oh my God. Wow. It's just so, horrible, and embarrassing.
STELLA. What is she doing here? Don't tell me what she's doing here, I can see what she's doing here. Get out of my house. GET HER OUT OF HERE.
CHARLIE. You have to go.
CLEA. Oh, look. I mean, this is horrible, right, but there's no reason to get all, like, rude. Things have happened here, obviously, but it's not like that's somebody's fault. I

mean, I am so not interested in some kind of a ridiculous scene.

(She stands and looks for her clothes.)

STELLA. Oh she's a brain surgeon isn't she? Yeah, this makes complete sense now. I can see why this happened.

CLEA. See this is what I'm talking about! People getting all insulting in a situation like this, why? Is that supposed to help? Because I don't think that is in the least bit helpful.

STELLA. Charlie, get her out of here!

CHARLIE. Clea. Just go.

CLEA. Why should I go? I mean, I was invited here. You and I are doing something here. You made a choice, Charlie, that involved me and not her, and that choice made you happy for the first time in whatever, I mean, you were like fucking miserable until I showed up.

STELLA. Why are you talking?

CLEA. I'm talking because I have something to say!

STELLA. You don't have anything to say! You don't know anything! And you're in my house! This is my house, I pay the rent here, that is my husband, you don't have any rights here!

CLEA. I've been fucking him all afternoon and you haven't. That doesn't exactly give me no rights.

(She sits on the couch, defiant. STELLA looks at CHARLIE, stunned.)

CHARLIE. I'm sorry. Clea. You have to go. We have things, Stella and I have things we need to — this shouldn't have happened, this way, at all, and, and —

CLEA. But it did happen. And you were the one who made it happen. So "should," I think "should" is a very useless word in a situation like this.

STELLA. Charlie?

CHARLIE. I'm sorry. I'm completely in the wrong.

CLEA. Stop. Just stop, already. "In the wrong?"

CHARLIE. *(Furious)* Clea, do not interfere in this!

CLEA. She's the one who's interfering! Come on, things were fine until she showed up!

CHARLIE. Stop acting like an idiot!

CLEA. You're the one who's being an idiot! "In the wrong?" You're just going to give away your power like that? To her? That's what she wants, that's what she's been about this whole time, I pay the rent, I want a baby, go suck up to stupid crazy Nick because me and my highlighters rule the world, what about what you want?

STELLA. Is that what you told her? This person, this, you told her — what did you tell her? Why do I care what you told her, that's clearly the least of, we're married, we've been married for —

CHARLIE. *(Overlap)* No. No, I did not tell her — this is not, this was not meant to be anything, Stella, this was a mistake —

STELLA. A mistake is forgetting my birthday, Charlie. I don't know what this is.

(She sits, desolate.)

CLEA. Charlie, are you coming?

CHARLIE. What?

CLEA. Look, we're doing something. Right? We were doing something, before she barged in.

STELLA. I live here! Are you insane? Because you sound insane. You're having an affair with an insane person. Maybe I'm the insane person, I can't, I don't even know, I have, there are — I don't, was your life that bad that you had to let this into it?

CHARLIE. No.

STELLA. Fourteen years, fourteen! You can just, for this? This thing, this isn't a person, even, I don't know what she is —

CLEA. Okay —

STELLA. You shut up! You've ruined my life, I don't have to take care of your feelings! Charlie, say something, please! What happened? Why did you do this? Was there some other way I should have been taking care of you?

CLEA. He's a man, he doesn't need a mommy.

STELLA. You know, I will hurt you. I will find some sort of weapon, there's got to be something somewhere, a knife or a vase, anything really is starting to look good, and I will hurt you and we will all end up in the Daily News. I promise you, I am not kidding. You need to get out of my house, right now. RIGHT NOW.

CLEA. Look at you, you don't even get it yet! You're just acting like a man, threatening violence and oh you're in charge of everything, why don't you just start waving your highlighters and screaming Heil Hitler? If you knew how to keep him, you would've. Look at him! He's just like totally silent around you. He's nobody with you. Let me tell you something, he isn't like that with me. With me, he's a lion, roaming the earth. With me, he's a god!

STELLA. You have got to be fucking kidding me.

CLEA. You don't make him feel the way I do. You don't

even begin to know how. So you can go ahead and hit me, or hurt me, or whatever, be violent, just like a man? But that's what your problem is. I'm going, Charlie. You know where to find me.

(She goes. There is a long moment of silence.)

STELLA. Why?

CHARLIE. Don't ask why.

STELLA. *(Suddenly furious.)* Don't ask — why? "Why" is off the table? You just completely—that was the most humiliating — I'm humiliated, Charlie! I'm, I'm everything is, my whole life is suddenly not even — and for that? And I'm not allowed to ask WHY?

CHARLIE. This is just, I can't — I can't...

STELLA. Stop being such a fucking coward and say something!

CHARLIE. You're too competent.

(There is a silence at this.)

STELLA. What?

CHARLIE. Everything. Gets done. Even when you hate what you're doing, you get it done. You're like a machine. Everything gets done.

STELLA. *(Almost in tears, suddenly.)* I'm not a machine. That's a lie.

CHARLIE. You're coherent. Everything coheres, and I, I can't — anymore — because I'm — and you're perfect. Your feelings are perfect. Your work is perfect. You hold down a job you think is stupid and it frustrates you in the perfect way.

Even in how you're not perfect, even in how things get to you, you're just, even your neurosis is perfect. You're so fucking competent, you don't ever expect too much out of life. You handle all of it. Even this. Even this! I'm watching you — you're handling it. You're already going to forgive this. THAT WAS A FOREGONE CONCLUSION. And then I'll have that, too. Your competence, and your forgiveness. Oh and your money, let's not forget that.

STELLA. So this is my fault?

CHARLIE. *(Snarling)* No! It's my fault! It's my crime! And I own it! It's the only thing you left me, the ability to fuck up, and I want it! It's mine! This fucking disaster is mine, and you can just keep your fucking hands off of it!

STELLA. I don't understand why this is happening. Why are you talking to me like this?

CHARLIE. I'm talking to you like this because this is who I am! And I'm sick of pretending to be perfect, like you, because that is not the person I want to be!

STELLA. This is some sort of fucking mid-life crisis. You want to fuck idiotic twenty somethings because that's what everybody else does, there isn't even a shred of originality in this —

CHARLIE. I wasn't looking for originality, Stella. I was looking to feel like someone who still had a shred of life in him!

STELLA. And fucking great looking idiots is the only way you can do that? Are you kidding me? I mean it. You don't like your life so you honestly think that screwing that girl — that girl who can hardly speak — who has no character or substance or anything — that that is going to do something, for you, make you whole, make you understand who you are in the world —

CHARLIE. I don't want that. Don't you understand?

STELLA. This is just, it's just self-loathing, Charlie! You're projecting your self loathing all over the rest of us and destroying everything so you can destroy yourself —

CHARLIE. Thanks, Stell, that's really, this is a thrilling moment to be psychoanalyzed —

STELLA. What else am I supposed to do?

CHARLIE. Nothing! Don't do anything! And don't explain this because I don't want to understand it! I just want to feel something. Remember when you felt things?

STELLA. I feel things!

CHARLIE.You feel unhappy. You feel competent. You feel like a wall.

STELLA. Don't you tell me what I feel. I feel disgust!

CHARLIE. You know what? She's right about one thing. If you want me to stay, you really don't know the first thing about how to make that happen.

(He heads for the door.)

STELLA. Where are you going?

CHARLIE. I'm going to a party.

(He slams the door. Blackout.)

Scene 5

(STELLA and LEWIS, in LEWIS'S apartment.)

STELLA. Thanks for letting me come over, I...

LEWIS. No, sure, thanks for calling. You look great.

STELLA. I look like shit.

LEWIS. Well, no. You feel like shit. But you look, great. Come on in, come on in.

STELLA. Have you heard from him?

LEWIS. No.

STELLA. Do you know where he is?

LEWIS. Stella...

STELLA. Is he living with her?

LEWIS. I don't know. That seems...

STELLA. I know, but where else would he be?

LEWIS. I don't know.

STELLA. How did this happen? So fast? Didn't it happen so fast?

LEWIS. Yes. It did.

STELLA. Did you know it was going on?

LEWIS. I...

STELLA. You did.

LEWIS. I thought, there was one night, here, a couple weeks ago. I thought something might...

STELLA. How long ago?

LEWIS. A couple weeks. Three weeks?

STELLA. Was it going on, then, is that what you mean? He was already, three weeks ago?

LEWIS. I don't know. Maybe it started that night, I don't — do you really want to —

STELLA. Yes. Yes! I want to, I can't — there's so much, you go, we had a good marriage. I thought. There was so much bile, when he, I'm too competent. That's what he told me. With so much hatred, I didn't.... I thought he loved me.

LEWIS. He does love you.

STELLA. He's gone, Lewis! I called his cell phone, a bunch of times. I left utterly humiliating messages, please call, please come home, we have to talk, and and and nothing. I don't even know where he is. Do you think he's with her? Why would he be with that person?

LEWIS. I don't know.

STELLA. I mean I guess she's pretty. She's just so — but she is pretty. Is that enough?

LEWIS. No.

STELLA. Do you think she's pretty?

LEWIS. No.

STELLA. But she's attractive. She's sexy.

LEWIS. No.

STELLA. I walked in on them. Did he tell you?

LEWIS. I haven't spoken to him.

STELLA. Then how do you know where he is?

LEWIS. I don't, Stella. Sweetie. I don't know.

STELLA. I know, I'm sorry, I'm sorry, I shouldn't be dumping this on you.

LEWIS. That's not —

STELLA. I should go. I should go home. I'm afraid to go home. I don't know where my husband is.

(She starts to cry. LEWIS goes to her, puts his arm around her. She sobs into his shirt.)

LEWIS. I would like to kill him.

STELLA. No. It's okay. It's not okay, it's so confusing. I'm sorry, I don't want to get snot on your sweater.

LEWIS. It's okay. I'm going to get you a glass of wine.

(He GOES. STELLA sits alone for a moment. She starts to cry again, then dries her eyes, shakes herself. She reaches into her purse and pulls out a manila envelope. She sets it on the coffee table, then takes it back and holds it to her chest. LEWIS RETURNS, carrying two glasses. He sees her, takes a moment, then proceeds.)

LEWIS. *(Continuing)* Hey.

STELLA. Oh. Thank you. I'm sorry about all this, Lewis. I just didn't, I needed to see you and think about how normal my life was, when something like this happens, all of a sudden everything you thought you knew, it's all, I'm too competent. Did you know? I didn't know. I'm too —

LEWIS. Sweetie, there's nothing wrong with you. He's going through something, it doesn't have anything to do with you. You're perfect.

STELLA. That's what he said. That's why he hates me now.

LEWIS. He doesn't hate you.

STELLA. Oh god I'm sorry I'm being such a, oh, I don't want to drown in self-pity, that's so repulsive, I hate it when people do that. I'm just very confused.

LEWIS. Have some wine.

STELLA. *(With a shred of irony.)* Yes, that will help, won't it. Alcohol is so useful when you just want to clear your head.

(She takes a drink.)

LEWIS. *(Cautious)* What's that?

(He points to the envelope.)

    STELLA. It's the baby.
    LEWIS. What?
    STELLA. My baby. They sent me, when you do these international adoptions, they send you pictures, when they've picked out your baby. So. They sent me pictures of my baby.

(Upset, but trying to stay on top of it now, she tries to open the envelope. She can't manage it.)

    LEWIS. Here. Let me.
    STELLA. I'm sorry.

(LEWIS opens the envelope and takes out several photographs, and a document of several pages.)

    LEWIS. She's beautiful.
    STELLA. Isn't she beautiful?
    LEWIS. Beautiful.
    STELLA. She's, they send you that packet, when they pick your baby — I just told you this already, I'm sorry, I started doing that — repeating myself all the time — like my mother, my crazy mother does that —
    LEWIS. Does Charlie know...
    STELLA. I told him. I mean, I called him, and I told him. That we have to let them know. If we want her or not. I left a message on his cell phone.
    LEWIS. And he didn't...
    STELLA. No. Nothing. *(Beat)* I don't know what's happened. To my life.

LEWIS. You can do it anyway. Can't you? You went through the whole process. They approved you.

STELLA. They approved both of us, and I don't know where he is! I don't know where that girl lives, I even tried to track her down through the stupid temp agency and they wouldn't give me the information and I told them off and canceled our contract with them. I did. Without consulting anyone, I just — I'm acting like a crazy person and I don't care. I would go over there and beg him, just — how can I, I would anyway, my pride is, I don't care. Do think this is why? That he didn't want the baby?

LEWIS I don't know why, Stella. You want my opinion, he's completely lost his mind, leaving you for anybody for any length of time is just about the most insane thing I've ever heard of. Ever.

STELLA I'm not going to be able to get her. Am I. They won't give her to me, now. And all I'll have, ever, is that stupid job that I hate, I hate that job —

LEWIS. You'll get her.

STELLA. Nothing. All I'll ever have, is nothing.

(She is utterly bewildered with grief. LEWIS sits there, bereft for a moment.)

LEWIS. *(Blurting)* It's my fault.

STELLA. Oh, Lewis, don't be ridiculous.

LEWIS. It's true. All of this, with Charlie, he didn't even — when he met her, he couldn't stand her. I was the one who brought her into our lives —

STELLA. No — she was just there —

LEWIS. I did, I asked her over. Because I didn't care, I knew that she was, some kind of succubus, and I wanted her anyway, that's why he even saw her again, he wouldn't have, if it wasn't for me. He wouldn't have.

STELLA. *(Beat)* You asked her...what did you ask her?

LEWIS. *(Beat)* Nothing.

STELLA. Your apartment? You said that before. She was in your apartment. Because you were on a date with her?

LEWIS. No. I mean, it doesn't matter. It doesn't...

STELLA. Well, what was she doing here, then? If you weren't on a date with her?

LEWIS. I was just, you know, I invited her over for a drink.

STELLA. And Charlie, you invited him over —

LEWIS. No, he just came by. And... she was there.

STELLA. Because you invited her.

LEWIS. Yes.

STELLA. Why did you invite her?

LEWIS. I know, it was stupid, I just —

STELLA. You wanted to, to fuck her.

LEWIS. No! Well, of course I — Stella, this isn't — useful —

STELLA. Useful! And being useful has worked so fucking well for me up to this point! She was here because you, you wanted her too, that monster, I mean, she is just a fucking nightmare — of a human being — and that didn't matter, did it —

LEWIS. Stella, this isn't, there's no point to this —

STELLA. THERE'S NO POINT TO ANYTHING, LEWIS, HAVEN'T YOU NOTICED? I'm sorry. I know, I'm being, I don't have to apologize, to you, you ruined my life —

LEWIS. I didn't, you know I —

STELLA. Fucking men, you fucks, you always stick together —

LEWIS. That is not —

STELLA. Not what, not useful? Christ. My head is going to explode. You and Charlie. Want her. Want her. That's what men want.

LEWIS. It isn't! You are what I wanted, but I couldn't have you because you're married to my best friend!

STELLA. *(Reeling)* Stop it, you liar, you're a fucking liar!

LEWIS. *(Furious)* It's true, you know it is, that's why I invited her —

STELLA. You invited her because — fuck you, who cares why you did it. You just did it —

LEWIS. Stella — *(Overlap)* Okay, you have to —Stella —

STELLA. Fuck you, fuck you, you invited her in, why, why was she here for him to see again, why was she here, it was because you — you were the one —

LEWIS. No —

STELLA. You just said it yourself! I have to get out of here. I have to go. I can't...I can't...

LEWIS. Stella —

STELLA. Shut up. Shut up. Don't talk to me. Don't ever talk to me again.

(She takes her pictures and papers, clutches them to herself, and goes. Blackout.)

Scene 6

(CLEA'S apartment. It is a mess. CHARLIE lies on the couch. There is a big bottle of vodka on the floor next to him. He pours himself a very stiff drink — a huge drink — which finishes off the bottle.)

CHARLIE. *(Calling)* We need more vodka!
CLEA. What?
CHARLIE. *(To himself.)* We need more vodka.

(He drinks, then —)

CHARLIE. *(Continuing; calling.)* So what'd you think of Nick?
CLEA. *(Off)* What?
CHARLIE. *(Yelling)* Nick. I saw you talking to him. At that party last night.

(CLEA ENTERS, dressed in black, to go out. She is jazzed, happy.)

CLEA. I thought he was fine.
CHARLIE. He's an asshole.
CLEA. Well, that's a little reductive.
CHARLIE. Reductive?
CLEA. *(Friendly)* Yeah, you know, like, reductive. Reductive. Like, judgmentally reductive.
CHARLIE. It's judgmentally reductive to call an asshole an asshole?
CLEA. *(Cheerful)* Look I don't even know the guy. I just

think defining any human being by one word, one demeaning sort of reducing word is something I don't want to be involved with.

(She hunts under the couch for shoes.)

CHARLIE. Yes, you have very high moral standards.
CLEA. I'm not trying to be judgmental! That's what I'm saying!
CHARLIE. Do you even know what reductive means?
CLEA. Somebody's in a bad mood....

(She leans over and kisses him. He starts to drag her back onto the couch, but she pulls away.)

CLEA. *(Continuing)* Oooooooh, I can't, Charlie. I have this thing I have to do.

(She slips on her heels, then goes to the wall, picks up make-up and jewelry off a bookcase there and finishes getting ready to go out.)

CHARLIE. What thing?
CLEA. It's like a dinner thing, with one of my girl-friends. I told you about it.
CHARLIE. Yeah, but all you say is it's a "thing." It's not exactly specific. It's like the opposite of specific. The only way you could say less is to say nothing at all.
CLEA. Which I know you would think was just fabulous since you think the way I talk is so stupid.

(He grabs her.)

CHARLIE. You look like a spider tonight. Getting ready to go out and sting some poor unsuspecting but delicious victim —

(He starts to kiss her. She pulls away.)

CLEA. Charlie, wow, you know, this is, you are acting, I think you have had a little too much vodka or something.

CHARLIE. We're out of vodka.

CLEA. That's not exactly a surprise. I mean, the way you've been sucking it down lately is a little —

(Beat.)

CHARLIE. No, go on.

CLEA. I am not criticizing. I mean, obviously you were in a very wrong place with the Nazi priestess and that was totally sucking you dry for how many years, I think it is obvious that I have had a lot of sympathy for you coming out of that situation, and I have been very supportive even through all this self-undermining behavior because of what you've been through.

CHARLIE. You never liked Stella, did you. Met her for fifteen minutes and you just couldn't stand her.

CLEA. Need I point out, neither can you.

CHARLIE. You don't know anything about anything.

CLEA. Oh brother. This is exactly what I mean about the vodka. No one made you do anything. You were very clear about what you wanted from this situation! Do you not recall saying to me, you just wanted to be clear?

CHARLIE. Yes I recall that.
CLEA. Well.

(She finds her purse and starts to go.)

CHARLIE. Can I borrow twenty bucks?

(She turns at this, startled.)

CHARLIE. *(Continuing)* We need more vodka.
CLEA. You want to borrow money? From me? For vodka?
Like, I don't have a job.
CHARLIE. Neither do I.
CLEA. So use a credit card.

(She starts to go again.)

CHARLIE. She cut them off. None of them work anymore.

(CLEA turns on this, startled.)

CLEA. I just — wait a minute. All of your credit cards?
You have like six.
CHARLIE. All of them. None of them. Work.
CLEA. The Nazi priestess —
CHARLIE. Stopped them.
CLEA. So you don't have any money.
CHARLIE. Nope.
CLEA. Well, what does she expect you to live on?
CHARLIE. Not her, apparently.

CLEA. What a bitch.

CHARLIE. What did you say?

CLEA. Well, it's just so passive-aggressive.

CHARLIE. I think cutting off all my credit cards would be considered aggressive-aggressive, Clea.

CLEA. Which is why you're not with her. So, look — *(Digs in her purse.)* I don't have a lot of money because as you know I just came here a few months ago, from Ohio,

CHARLIE. *(Overlap)* Ohio, you don't say.

CLEA. And I have not yet found a job that I think is something I could really get excited about but I do have some money. My mom sends me a check once in a while. Here. I mean, that is terrible, what she did.

(She holds out a bill. CHARLIE stares at it, takes a breath, then takes it, looks at it.)

CHARLIE. This is a ten.

CLEA. Well, I don't have a ton of money, Charlie, I think that's obvious. And due respect, given what I've gone through with my mother, I don't really want to just give you all my money, to just get drunk with.

CHARLIE. Not that you're judging.

CLEA. Well — you don't — like — expect me to support you now? You don't expect that, do you?

CHARLIE. No. I don't.

(He pockets the bill, and downs the rest of the vodka. She watches him, uncomfortable.)

CLEA. So, like — where are you going to live, now?

CHARLIE. *(A beat.)* Are you kicking me out?

CLEA. Well, I think it's obvious that you can't stay here forever.

CHARLIE. Not to argue semantics, because that is in fact a dicey proposition with the likes of you, Clea — but there is a rather large difference between "forever" and "now."

CLEA. You're so drunk, I can't even talk to you.

CHARLIE. I'm not drunk. I wish I was drunk but unfortunately *(Yelling, suddenly.)* WE ARE OUT OF VODKA.

(She stares at him, shocked.)

CLEA. Did you just raise your voice to me?

CHARLIE. Why, yes I did.

CLEA. *(Hushed and pious.)* Because that is — unacceptable. I do not yell. No one in my family ever yells. That is not something I can accept in any way.

CHARLIE. Soooo...stealing other people's husbands for the sheer fun of being a bitch is okay, but RAISING YOUR VOICE is pretty much crossing the line.

CLEA. *(High and mighty.)* I am asking you to leave.

CHARLIE. Yeah, we'll get to that in good time, I'm sure, but I have a question first. Who you going out with? Are you going out with Nick?

CLEA. *(Caught, tossed.)* That is just — I'm going out with friends! I told you!

CHARLIE. *(Yelling now.)* So cheating on me with that shithead NICK is all right, but YELLING IS OFF THE TABLE.

CLEA. Cheating on you? CHEATING? This exclusive and, and proprietary language is really so retro —

CHARLIE. Call it whatever you want —

CLEA. You were the one who wanted to be clear!

CHARLIE. *(Furious, yelling.)* All right then, as long as we're arguing semantics, why don't we just call it lying? Is that okay? Lying to my face while you go off to fuck my total nemesis?

CLEA. Like you even care —

CHARLIE. MEN ACTUALLY DO CARE ABOUT THAT SHIT, CLEA.

CLEA. You have to leave! This yelling is terrible! I am not a violent person and I do not accept it in the people I care about!

CHARLIE. That's easy enough to pull off, because you don't care about anybody! Do you? It's fantastic! You look like that, you screw like a bunny, and you have no soul! Seriously. It is awe inspiring. That no soul thing? You make it quite, it's very seductive. Letting go. Forgetting that you ever wanted anything else. Because what else is there? Except looking like that. Being hot shit. At a really great party. Inside the void.

(He stands on the bed, lost inside himself.)

CLEA. I don't know what the fuck you are talking about.

CHARLIE. What are the odds?

CLEA. Well, I cannot have insane people living in my apartment and just yelling at me, whenever they feel like it. Here's another ten.

(She reaches into her purse, holds out another bill. CHARLIE stares at it.)

CLEA. *(Continuing)* Take it.

(CHARLIE does not take it. She finally throws it on the ground.)

CLEA. *(Continuing)* I don't care if you take it or not, you crazy loser. But you better not be here when I get back. Or I'm calling the cops.

(She goes. After a moment, CHARLIE reaches down and takes the money, pockets it. Blackout.)

Scene 7

(A remote corner of a party. STELLA is there, with CHARLIE. He is a mess. They stare at each other for a long moment of silence.)

CHARLIE. Hi.
STELLA. Charlie, wow. Edward didn't tell me he had invited you. I didn't think, we asked so many people if they knew where you, where you —
CHARLIE. No. I just heard from someone, you know, I bumped into a friend of his on the street, and he mentioned that Edward was, you know... you know, you look great. How have you been?
STELLA. How have I *been*? Terrific. Being abandoned by my husband was a trial at first but over time it forced me to do some real soul searching and I think I've grown as a result.
CHARLIE. You're still working for that talk show.

STELLA. Oh for heavens's sake. It's been months, Charlie. You disappear for months, and now you just show up like like like — did you get my messages at all? I left like, a hundred messages, maybe, on your cellphone. Didn't you – did —

CHARLIE. Yeah. I got them. For a while. I mean, my cell doesn't work anymore. They cut it off, when I stopped paying. When you stopped paying.

STELLA. Well, what was I supposed to do? I didn't know if you were dead or alive, or if, or if —

CHARLIE. *(Overlap)* No, you did the right thing. You should have cut me off, long before you did. You did the right thing.

STELLA. You look like shit.

CHARLIE. Yeah, right. Right? *(Beat)* Look, can I borrow a few bucks?

STELLA. What?

CHARLIE. I'm really broke. I mean, it's temporary, but a few bucks would really help right now. There's a kind of housing situation...

STELLA. A housing — where are you living Charlie?

CHARLIE. I'm with friends! Mostly.

STELLA. Charlie. Are you homeless?

CHARLIE. No, I'm with friends! I said, I'm with friends. It's okay. If you don't have any on you, that's all right. I'll pay you back.

STELLA. Why didn't you come home?

CHARLIE. *(A beat, then.)* I wrecked it. It wasn't there anymore. It wasn't what I wanted. I thought nothing would be better.

STELLA. Is it?

(LEWIS APPEARS, with STELLA'S wrap. He doesn't see CHARLIE at first.)

LEWIS. Sorry that took so long. To get to the wraps I had to get by three girls who were throwing up, and one who was shooting up.
CHARLIE. Edward's parties are great, aren't they?
LEWIS. A total blast.
CHARLIE. Hey, Lewis.

(He reaches over; they shake.)

LEWIS. Charlie. *(To STELLA.)* You okay?
CHARLIE. *(Distracted)* Yeah, great! I mean, I was hoping to find Clea here, but she's, who knows where she is... I'm telling you, she's really a piece of work. You were so better off out of that. I did you a favor, man, I really did.
LEWIS. *(To STELLA, quiet.)* Do you want to go? We can go, right now.
STELLA. I don't know.
CHARLIE. No, God, come on, I can find Clea later, it's so great to see you guys! You look great. Stell, you look terrific.
LEWIS. *(To STELLA.)* We should go.
CHARLIE. *(Snapping)* She's my wife! Would you stop telling her what to do! I mean what the fuck are you...what... what the fuck is this?

(A beat.)

STELLA. We're going to China, Charlie. Next week. Lewis and I are going to China to get my baby.

CHARLIE. Together?

STELLA. Yes. Lewis and I are going to China together.

CHARLIE. Well, that's just — classic. How long did you wait, huh, Lewis? A week, two weeks, how long did it take you to start moving in on my wife?

STELLA. You have no right to even ask —

CHARLIE. How long did it take you, Lewis?

LEWIS. Three weeks.

CHARLIE. Three weeks! Wow, that's, you know, admirable self-restraint. You know, you really gave it time then. Good for you. Three weeks. That was loyal.

LEWIS. You're not allowed to expect loyalty after what you did!

CHARLIE. Not from you, clearly!

LEWIS. This is such a distortion.

CHARLIE. Make your excuses! You stole my wife.

STELLA. He didn't steal me.

CHARLIE. Oh yeah, he loves you. He really really loves you, that's really what's going on here. Love will find a way. I'm so happy for you both.

STELLA. *(Furious at this.)* Well, what was I supposed to do, wait for you? Wait for you to to — come to your senses and and — what was I supposed to do? You just threw me away like it was nothing, Charlie! How could you? How could you. Neither of us were perfect, but what we had was real.

CHARLIE. I DON'T WANT ANYTHING *REAL*. Where do you, where where do you think you are, anyway? Have you been out of the house lately? Have you been to Times

Square? It's fantastic! You look up, and they're everywhere. Movie stars. TV stars. Underwear models. Those crazy rap people nobody understands, they're everywhere. Three and four stories tall, hovering over everything, like gods. Laughing. All of them, *laughing* at us. Because they know. All these fake people are having a more real life than we are! Real? Why should I want to be real? Fuck reality.

(She turns, away from him, upset. CHARLIE starts toward her; LEWIS steps between them.)

    LEWIS. Leave her alone Charlie. Leave us alone.

(He takes her hand leads her off, back to the party.)

    CHARLIE. Wait. Wait wait wait.

(Silence. He paces, restless, tries to go back into the party, fails. Completely alone now, he looks out at the night. After a moment, CLEA ENTERS, in a beautiful black dress.)

    CLEA. I heard you were looking for me. I saw the Nazi Priestess and your friend; they looked pretty cozy. Anyway, they told me in front of Nick that you were out here looking for me and I have to say it's really a problem, okay? I mean, Nick is completely allergic to you now because that lunch you had, you weren't exactly subtle. So make it fast.
    CHARLIE. I need that money.
    CLEA. What?

CHARLIE. We racked up a lot on my credit cards. I need that money back. Fifteen hundred, at least. To start.

CLEA. Fifteen hundred dollars? I don't even know you!

CHARLIE. You know me. You spent all my money. You took me from my wife. You're here with my ex-friend Nick —

CLEA. "Ex-friend," who you always called "the asshole —"

CHARLIE. *(Anger rising.)* He *is* an asshole!

CLEA. *(Sharp)* Well, that asshole is my *boss.* I am his personal assistant.

CHARLIE. And what did you have to do to get *that* plum job?

CLEA. I did pretty much the same thing I did for you, only this time, it *got* me somewhere. And Nick has been really great to me. I can't be seen with you.

(She starts to go. He steps in front of her.)

CHARLIE. Wait wait wait —

CLEA. Get out of my way, Charlie —

CHARLIE. No wait! Forget about the money. Please, I just to talk to someone for a second, I'm out there by myself all day and I I, Lewis and Stella were here and they left, and I just can't go back down there by myself. I can't go back down.

(He doesn't move. She sighs, frustrated.)

CLEA. Oh boy. Look. I'm sorry you're like not having a good time right now, I really really am. Now get out of my way.

CHARLIE. Because, to be that alone. People everywhere, and no one who sees you. With recognition. It's you!

CLEA. Okay. Earth to Charlie

(He takes her by the arm and leads her back to the railing.)

CHARLIE. And I'm just starting to see, just now even, what's wrong with all of this, this fall into narcicissm —

CLEA. CHARLIE.

CHARLIE. Is how lonely it is. Aren't you lonely?

CLEA. *(Startled)* Am I what?

CHARLIE. Lonely. That's the problem. That's what's wrong with it. All of it. We're not meant to be this lonely, and you and I, we, we went to this lonely place together, and I just think that, I know, there's nothing between us, but maybe — we could, we could help each other out of it. If we just had a cup of coffee. Or even, not even a cup of coffee. Maybe just a glass of water. If we started that simply, and had a glass of water. Together.

CLEA. You want me to have a glass of water with you?

CHARLIE. It might help. Holy beggars did this. They just ate and drank the simplest, people would give them what they could, from the earth, and it was like a connection.

CLEA. This isn't funny.

CHARLIE. To the self, and others, connection for people who have no place in the world. Which none of us, really, none of us do.

CLEA. Let go of my hand.

CHARLIE. No, listen — To my heart. Listen —

CLEA. I said LET GO!

(She shoves him away, steely.)

CLEA. Get it together, would you? God, you're a mess, you're really just a total wreck and there's a party going on in there, Charlie! Get a clue! There's four casting agents in there! Plus Nick — okay I'm going to tell you this I don't know why because you so don't deserve it but the fact is, he still needs somebody to play the homeless guy in the third act and it's only two lines and I could get him to just give it to you if you would just — just tell Nick how much you love the pilot, he will really like that. You know part of the reason he gets so edgy with you is because he thinks you're really talented, like fucked up but talented and honestly, if you just said some nice things it would solve everything! Just don't talk about having a glass of water with him, okay? That is too nuts. Holy beggars, also off the table, okay? Okay, Charlie? Honestly, you are so much work, I'm going to have to have a massage for a week to get over this. I mean it. It's a party! Okay, Charlie? It's a party.

(She pushes by him, back into the party. CHARLIE watches her go, then looks out over the water.)

CHARLIE. It is surreal. That's exactly what it is.

(He leans back, looking into the doorway, considering whether or not he will RE-ENTER the fray. Blackout. End of play.)

The Clean House
By Sarah Ruhl
2005 Pulitzer Prize Finalist

This extraordinary new play by an exciting new voice in the American drama was runner-up for the Pulitzer Prize. The play takes place in what the author describes as "metaphysical Connecticut", mostly in the home of a married couple who are both doctors. They have hired a housekeeper named Matilde, an aspiring comedian from Brazil who's more interested in coming up with the perfect joke than in house-cleaning. Lane, the lady of the house, has an eccentric sister named Virginia who's just nuts about house-cleaning. She and Matilde become fast friends, and Virginia takes over the cleaning while Matilde works on her jokes. Trouble comes when Lane's husband Charles reveals that he has found his soul mate, or "bashert" in a cancer patient named Anna, on whom he has operated. The actors who play Charles and Anna also play Matilde's parents in a series of dream-like memories, as we learn the story about how they literally killed each other with laughter, giving new meaning to the phrase, "I almost died laughing." This theatrical and wildly funny play is a whimsical and poignant look at class, comedy and the true nature of love. 1m, 4f (#6266)

"Fresh, funny ... a memorable play, imbued with a somehow comforting philosophy: that the messes and disappointments of life are as much a part of its beauty as romantic love and chocolate ice cream, and a perfect punch line can be as sublime as the most wrenchingly lovely aria." — *NY Times*